Points In the Network

poems by

Gabrielle Myers

Finishing Line Press
Georgetown, Kentucky

Points In the Network

Copyright © 2025 by Gabrielle Myers
ISBN 979-8-89990-214-7 First Edition
All rights reserved under International and Pan-American Copyright Conventions. No part of this book may be reproduced in any manner whatsoever without written permission from the publisher, except in the case of brief quotations embodied in critical articles and reviews.

ACKNOWLEDGMENTS

Edible East Bay: "Live as the Tomatillo Reaches for Life on a Hot July Day," Fall 2022

Thank you to Leah and Kevin Maines, Christen Kincaid, and the *Finishing Line Press* team for making *Points in the Network* possible!

Publisher: Leah Huete de Maines
Editor: Christen Kincaid
Cover Art: Jill McLennan
Author Photo: Kora Centro del Contemporaneo
Cover Design: Elizabeth Maines McCleavy

Order online: www.finishinglinepress.com
                also available on amazon.com

                          Author inquiries and mail orders:
                              Finishing Line Press
                                 PO Box 1626
                           Georgetown, Kentucky 40324
                                    USA

Contents

Fueling Never Dissipates 1
Memory—Rockville, Maryland, 1986 2
Grandma Ginny Gets Going 3
Prediction 4
Resonance 5
On a Run with Ghostie 6
To Spring Rise 7
She Didn't Fit, Until 8
Spring into Summer 9
Summer Memory 10
Spring Wind from California 11
Togetherness in Spring 12
More 13
Time Medicine 14
The Pattern 17
Be Not Afraid 18
In June 19
Fullness 20
Map Dream 21
Stop Time 22
Enough 23
Horribleness Sparks Creation 24
The Many Selves Within One 25
Summer Ballad 26
What We Are Never 27
Not Felt as One But Two 28
East 19th Street Elegy 29
Awakening 30
Live as the Tomatillo Reaches for Life 31
Words are No Use 32
Aperture 33
The Hive in Us Strives 34
Destiny's Garment 35
Shrouded Silence's Heat 36
The Joining 37
Put summer into these lines 38

Each Tremble Becomes an Earthquake 39
Autumn and Embracing a Never Wane 40
Time Reverses While We Sleep 41
Ash Flakes Linger like Substantial Fragments 42
Smoked Summer 43
Queens of La Luna Bella 44
Conflagration 45
Love's Perpetual Birth 46
Filter, Dissolve, Cut, Cycle 47
Concoct 48
No Lull, No Stop-Time 49
Bildungsroman 50
Mural on Balmy Alley, San Francisco 51
Rise to Elevation 52
Water's Benediction 53
Swallows' Calls Rising 54
Ripe in Our Apex 55
Diverge from Difference's Narrative 56
Rust New Forms 57
Image Focus 58
Channel the Void's Roar 59
Pitch Our Words, Pitch Our Minds 60
Don't Stop 61
Elegy for Her Promise 62
To the Homeless Man Asleep Across the Street 63
Walk Ourselves Free 64
Second Berry Harvest 65
From the Powered Center 66
Stretch In Ascension 67
Beach Day 68
Summon Sheets That Will Swallow Dryness 69
No Escape Needed 70
End of the Fire Season, End of the Dry Season Ode 71
Suddenness 72

"As if the sky were a pattern of nerves and our thoughts and memories traveled across it."
Louise Erdrich, *Love Medicine*

"Lean under the weight of what is real"
Claudia Rankine, *Citizen*

"It was something about how life will break you. How that's the reason we're here, and to go sit by an apple tree and listen to the apples fall and pile around you, wasting all that sweetness."
Tommy Orange, *There, There*

Fueling Never Dissipates

What makes us turn in our bed sheets,
our bellies, backs, sides filled
with movement, the itch to climb?
How did fueling never dissipate
as years turned, as days merged with nights in accumulation?
Ecstasy and excitement breathe energy through blinds;
we take sunlight and feel its curve
through our bodies—uncontainable.
Unstoppable, our amazement to meet a grass blade in growth,
smell honeysuckle as it pushes beyond
green lid, casts sweetness
for a hummingbird to sip and suck.

Memory—Rockville, Maryland

Crickets throb and pulse, a clock's
tick ringing with my breath.
Water rushes from a thunderstorm the night before,
washes into creek's red clay edges—
runs smooth, burnt red.
Everything around us
—clay and soil drying on the short trail,
small sticks poking from grey mud,
bamboos' thin giving rods, needle-like leaves,
tulip poplars' delicate flower cups and fat leaves,
crayfish under a steel plank covering the creek's edge,
crickets and cicadas in their itchy melodies,
my breath, a humid swell—all lift
from this fecundity, a cradle
that launches us forward in time.

Grandma Ginny Gets Going

She pushes the sun, hands aflame, lilts like a jay
In its morning call, leaves the house she held for years.
She dives down through losses that move away like gardens
Where row after row of raspberries and blueberries ripen.
Light makes berries into sweet bags, fills her mouth
So that her blood runs thick with fruit juice.
Like a vine fed by rain she curls and twists,
Looks over The Valley like a hawk, swoops down, plucks.

Even in death, she flies, persists as always.
Her father's disowning her,
Son's stroke or daughter's insanity
Don't follow her too hard in the head.
Every morning, she gets up, makes fresh squeezed OJ and toast.
Too tough to let blows take her down, she surges,
Takes each day, ascends.

Prediction

We're like kiwi vines opening to spring sun
We bend and unfurl to grasp all light
While swallows dance their awakening nets
While saturated soil sings with water sifting
While ants and crickets begin gathering.

We feel emergence vibrate like broad leaves,
Elongate, expand against our bark-like skin,
Push into gathering light.

Resonance

If you stand, face
those voices whose words soar to steel roofs—
if you shout words of gentleness,
how can all ears not lean to hear you?

Speak back, swirl in a tunnel of reception;
syllables spin until they reach brain,
synapses catch resonance.

On a Run with Ghostie

Orange and lemon blossoms steady their fragrance
in weighted, before rain air. We run,
each step ignites my hamstring muscles,
each breath precious in its gift
after last night's strain. The German Shepherd, Ghostie,
pulls me forward with his leash, always intent
on smelling the next tree side and grass patch.
He jams his nose in, inhales all that the cinnamon scented bark,
bruised tender grass, and other dog pee can give.
Then the slight leg lift and pee—usually just three drops.
His lazy left eye, damaged
from a former owner or from birth,
looks down while his right stares up at me.
Each short city block we stop three times;
I stare at Victorian stairways, apartment entryways from the 70's,
onion and cardinal flower blossoms until I get bored,
impatient, and pull him along, saying
"Why do we have to stop at every tree, Ghostie?"

Even though he doesn't use words, he knows
what I mean. You can't stop and pee on everything
that you could possibly stop and pee on
because you'd run out of pee,
which has happened to Ghostie on many runs.
Often toward the end of our run,
he lifts his leg and not even a small drop emerges.
But he still pulls me left and right on sidewalks
all the way home, jams his nose
into camphor and sycamore bark,
smells switch grass and nasturtium essence,
inhales every particle of life that we pass.

To Spring Rise

In the middle of spring's rising
I withdraw into mind swirl and love fear
Three levels of bird cadence vibrate from ground to bush to tall canopy
Breeze carries winged insects and citrus blossoms
I want to feel rebirth's serenity and chaos
Be able to mimic what my straining eyes see and nose inhales
Desire to be set for new growth, bear untold fruits
With a heart resistant to blisters, with a mind spilling a waterfall
Even though caught in a heart return's swirling doubts
Everything goes back into a beginning
Like seemingly dead tree limbs cut back to their ends regrow
From what seems like nothing comes leaf shower, blossom rain
When one starts an outward journey
Wards off freezing winds and the mind's naysayers
The drive into another propels.

She Didn't Fit, Until

In this child's mind canopy, an endless shuffle,
under a blanket wedged on a bunk bed's side,
down in that makeshift cave she wonders.
Up she goes after an awareness hits,
into the world to hesitantly claim herself as a being
from an ignition, from the safety that was never there,
from a fear of what she might not become
or might merge with, a twisting and trembling
away from extinguishment, from boys
who bullied her because of short hair,
from girls who, makeup drenched, hid so much.

As a bird set on not being wing bound,
as a voice set on casting forward a sound,
she emerges, hums, enchants
with her hearing, with the need to speak,
be spoken to, confront undulating voices.
Whether speech be to burn, hurt, uplift,
or love, this girl's voice able to move
into a throng without losing frequency,
move into wholeness announcing
a convergence not being a loss but a charge.

Spring into Summer

Easy the days warm to spring's reassembling light,
slip into long hours open to receive sun's thunder.

Light pours down, fills all cracks,
exposes a spiderweb's shadow, lifts

with a thick finger into and over opened leaves,
leaves tepidity on hours' other side, indifferent

to mixed emotions. Full long into light's hours.
Full thrust into heat and stench
from a pressure released rotten tomato.

Full on into ripped shorts, worn
flip flops near lake, river, ocean water.
Dive into the crest, fold in sand,
hand, flower, fruit, leaf
—puncture into solstice's gifts.

Summer Memory

Crickets itch their pitches
Southern Magnolia spills bowling ball flowers
Crabgrass creates indecipherable networks beneath our feet
Hay fields throb with grasshoppers, mice, crows
Columns of coneflower, thistle, Queen Ann's lace, vetch, butterfly weed enlarge
Summer life smell: wet leaves decompose and turn to soil,
Ferns unfurl, stream water breathes under a willow,
Humidity gathers, lulls us into life

Spring Wind from California

Blow sycamore litter, still-born spring leaves
that didn't make the cut. Send pine needles and pollen
particles past our bungalows and Craftsman houses.
Comb in Pacific wave crests,
move them to bay, river, upstream to our inland sea.
Take smog that sits like a blanket of fog
in our fields, lift it up and over the Sierras,
push it east, beyond the Rockies' snow caps,
through Kansas corn tassels and thick soy stems in Missouri,
raise it over the Appalachians' blooming redbuds, over our stone
monuments, over the flooded Potomac to the Chesapeake,
beyond the Atlantic's bulges billowing toward release.

Togetherness in Spring

Thriving leaves surround us
let us dip our fingers into their fragile tenderness,
dig with our hands into soil
still wet from rainy season, tunnel
into each other like worms
spinning downward to bite decayed leaves.
Turn and be ushered into togetherness'
tension, how it can flare,
forever strengthened in perpetual bloom and fruit's knowledge;
slight dormancy only gives way to endurance,
a continual flushing, bearing forth, satiation.

Sparrows, seven per group, fly toward a sycamore.
A neighbor on either side of the street walks
his or her dog in opposite directions. Pollen particles,
blown into a light shaft, settle on our fence.
Baby ducks, their beaks firming, sip and splash
in a small pool. We can hear different ballads
fill the amber hour: hens discuss just thrown grubs,
neighbor's doves devour new grain,
crickets rub legs in a rosemary thicket.
Late afternoon's spoon
lifts spring into our being, soothes
with rest's sense inchoate action.

More

When an owl hoots, a train glides through,
pollen filters down, flies swirl outside,
then we know what it means to live in May's pressure
beneath striated clouds and dove serenade.

Nothing ever diminishes; in age, we feel more—
whether excitement in spring's warming soil or a love's turn,
let it throng and cluster, set to explode in our veins.

Time Medicine

I.
When wind picks up stray blossoms, tangles
itself into thin straw blades, she finds
a place to nest that part of herself capable
of fracture, division. Curl into a spot
between fierce gusts, as her nails' frayed edges
strengthen in shelter, as her brittle ends
fortify and begin to lengthen. Incubate the self
long enough to become whole again.
In the in-between spaces,
she will take back his fits, take back
her stumble toward the needle,
take back her son's loss—
reverse time by stopping herself in it.

II.
When earth turns and worms break soil,
push little bits to the side, cast their tang
into March air, then she knows it's time.
Tulips' naked heads break through compacted mulch,
plum blossoms whip like snowflakes
around her motion-filled body, and the winnowing starts.
To remove static, leap beyond what once was,
divide into a next version, revise,
rewrite, craft her life and what she sees again,
all of this will emerge from a shedding.

She was never a hot pan to the hand,
thin line pulled through a bill, So Co
straight on the rocks, "I don't give a damn"
on the outside of her mouth while inside the opposite
hunted her dreams like a racoon after a baby chicken.

Before that she was let loose
in fields behind her mom's apartment,
created a fort of branches, was a swordbearer
with a bamboo blade. Wonder at what might be pricked
her mind to imagine cities and people;
reframed her place in a world with new stores, new words,

less trash, palm trees' curling fronds,
sticky humidity causing skin to cling on benches.

What was familiar has muted into the rare now.
She hunts herself to believe again,
aims for ignorance of the last decade,
    to get to an unknowing,
        a start again; what would that be like?

    III.
    A hook-pull twists through her;
    a sudden gain in the loss
    of what she thought sturdy.
    Years spent in a cover
    of what she hated to love;
    years spent with a not yet,
    with his words spinning
    like a drain snake's sharp edges
    what she is, what he sees.
    To take that and turn into herself,
    move the hook-pull into her own hands,
    grip down and thrust her real self forward,
    launch that self away from fierce
    turn of fist and plate and word,
    she will. She will,
    through two kinds of violence
    mother herself long enough.

IV.
One afternoon after he twisted her hair into his blistered fists,
she ran into the field. Virginia summer thunderheads
billowed up like giant thumbs, small clouds flanked below
like her swollen palm. She lay in the field.
Among vetch, clover, Queen Ann's Lace,
a thistle's stubby growth pricked her back.
The clouds' steady moves, undulating across and behind each other,
their dipping into and out, layering, spinning toward her,
toward mountains, toward the valley
became a network that pulled her up into its vast net,

became energy webs that reached down to lift her up,
twist her into a nerve belly, synapse-spines
gathered to pulse and regeneration points.
She was not the woman who was here.
She was not, not that.
But she was that, was here
in this field after having run away from him.
She was, and was not that.
She was this also:
she was a point at this network's edge,
her soul and body lobbed up to meet, join it,
destruct and resurrect herself, lose herself,
not be and yet be her, and yet be a synapse
connected to the clouds' pulse,
at once.

The Pattern
After Grossman

Once held beyond fist, locked in reason,
caught in thin lines that hamper deciphering,
now logic spills forth uncontainable.
To know and not know, feel
and not be able to press logic into a word,
not be able to turn it in our guts long enough
to have words fall from our lips.
Syllables turn, our mouths lift in gaping openness;
ears pick whispered incantations
of a language familiar yet pushing our ears to processing's limit.
To take it in, to spin pronunciation
towards a synapse, what will it take?

Be Not Afraid

As a little girl in my bed in our suburban Maryland home, airplanes flying over our roof, their rumble and shingle shake, their boom through tulip poplar and bamboo forests, terrified me. The sound thrumming through the quiet 30 degrees, cloudy with no snow nights, lifted the 'me' up out of my body—this little girl's small feet blistered from running cross country for the Catholic Youth Organization, her hair that always got so tangled every night from tossing and turning, the burning in her belly from acid, stress, constant hunger, the blue down comforter held over her brown curls.

There is no me…well, there is because I am here, but fear and reality of someday not existing made me shake myself awake and turn on my side and pray to God to not let me die. I never want to stop existing. I never want to cease. Maybe it was growing up during the Cold War just a few miles from the DC border where talks of Three Mile Island and nuclear war filled dinner tables and classroom discussions.

Maybe it was being a latchkey kid with parents who left before 7 am and got home just after 7 pm, the stories of little girls stolen and brutalized and raped before they were thrown off to the side of some two-lane highway near Gaithersburg.

Maybe it was Marsha and Cindy, the two girls I went to junior high with who killed themselves to go meet Satan.

The newspapers must have had it wrong, they said it was the Slayer and thrash metal which told crazy curly haired and heavy eyelined Marsha to take Cindy's father's gun and shoot Cindy through the head, then turn the gun on her own mouth and pull.

How does one do that on a picnic table in Rock Creek Park's outer edge? I loved Slayer, headbanged to *South of Heaven*, and knew the papers were wrong.

Why would one ever want to end; why would one ever want to bring it on, the emptiness, quiet, ceasing?

Even now, with benign nodules in my lungs and thyroid that I watch like a pilot watches her radar navigation and compass, the airplane noise fear makes me turn over in bed, curl, bury my head in the comforter and pillow, touch my boyfriend's warm bare body with my palm—our house is no shield, no comfort from the inevitable.

In June

Again, the sun holds our feet to sidewalks
Lifts oak leaves and dew towards its gold
That inflates above tree limbs and rooftops
Where we once saw raindrops beat like tiny wings.

After short days and rain sinking into every crevice
Comes light stark and exposing; it lingers long and takes
Each soil crumb, rubs pollen into its corners,
Takes a sigh from the Bay, flings it over the Valley.

Then a loudness fills field and street corner, a humming
By crickets, birds, frogs, people flows uncontained,
Pulsates in a once still air, cascades noise
Full into our ears, our mouths.

Fullness

A fullness fills: what was once unfillable,
void-like, yields and yields, spills forth
fruit and vine. Now open,
no need of barrier or cocoon.
We can reach long into another, stretch
beyond what we thought we were
capable of. Forever carrying our womb,
protected by what gives us birth,
by what ventures out, out, out.

Map Dream

In her mind she imagines a map
textured with low points, ridges
spreading like horns on a ram's head.
She envisions fine road networks,
veined like webs on her hands, patterns
of journeys she took and has not taken,
town grids laid open
to how she might see them at 23, 31, 52,
how wood has been replaced with glass and concrete,
how burger stands have turned into smoothie stores.
Highways cut deep across flat lands,
level through solitary times where only she made
her days fillable, had to make a tree or a hill up
because if she didn't think it, it wasn't there.

If she were in this landscape now, not pushed
to land's edge, not gestating a mountain range,
she would collapse distances, run them
into the ocean so they feel a cold shock to awaken,
turn them in her mind's palm
like the dreams one has as a girl
that she never shakes through decades of traffic,
routine, exhaustive labor, empty bank accounts.
She would concoct a small road with no shoulders
that runs through a meadow thick
with flowers all fragrant in summer's gain
—a spring tunneling right through,
surging with water from mountain snow melt,
pooling on meadow's edge before overwhelming grasses,
ready to push beyond that border, filled with so much
of itself it can only overflow and cascade with force
on to the next place it will inhabit.

Stop Time

To have time to watch flies circle above the chicken pen,
watch their dance, turn, shift in slight wind, count them
to 18, shift focus to ash's thin new leaves
waving in a cool spring morning. Sit, be still,
think, but not too much, rest, let the mind pause,
sleep, breathe in clean air, dig dirt-stained nails
into soil, plant tomato, pepper, artichoke, basil,
again and again, run and be thankful
for each breath's blooming jasmine and honeysuckle,
cooking tomato sauce, frying garlic's sweet fragrances,
smell the earth awakening, feel lemon flower's pollen
sticky on hands, tomato vine resin holding fingers together,
inhale cilantro's tang, push into rotting zucchini blossoms,
lifted, gifted to arrive
at this stop time in between life's rush.

Enough

Clouds reflect helicopter noise;
For hours blade movement echoes
Through the city. Planes drone, choppers scissor
Dry air, ducks' splash, commuter trains ding.

A city drenched in spring's softness,
Plums fattening and rounding whole,
Tiny tomatoes form drops dense
As plywood, and two rivers rush
To their filling points before joining,
Pushing towards the Bay.

What safety holds us, what
Inevitability, what sureness allows
Our steps to be firm
In their movements towards each other?

Grip a day's motions;
Pen them down into our bellies,
Don't let their stitches slip.

Stillness and cloud, hemmed
In sun's safety without rain's threat.
Control the emptying, winnow it
To sliver points that slowly build until
Empathy grains fill and fill another's mind.

People pour over Capital Park to protest,
Pour over our commerce intersections;
Like coins we become numerous,
Make change by gathering each other.

Police cars speed by, four to a car in riot gear.
Above, three choppers spin to watch

Pressure to the neck, bullet in the side—
How does justice trickle down,
Invade every crevice of our city?

Horribleness Sparks Creation

Creators of this world,
our hands on keys, our voices able to shake walls,
let's place our fingers on levers and turn
a world most berated into one transformed and uplifted,
one where no one is kneed or shot because of difference
—one where degrading words have dissipated
into the atmosphere, become memory stones of a past
where we sung away all losses
we could not change, turned to what could be moved,
what could carry us forward into our ourselves,
all our selves chanting,
pulsing with perpetual beginning.

The Many Selves Within One

Bird song does not wrestle
with a freight truck's accelerating roar;
both sounds gestate a summer afternoon
where one closes eyes and dreams of a field,
of travel's congested movements,
of the energy it takes to carry a self to a new place,
a new way of processing a once familiar world.

A beat cultivates a rhythm,
creates a new order,
hums and changes molecules' behavior,
transfixes that which slithers and springs.
Know a self before it shifts;
get to the knowing as someone
you only have three days with,
prod with curiosity the barriers,
limits, far-ranging sensations.
Look with wonder at a leaf's ridge,
an ear's fold, the adamant restraint
that appears without reason.

Summer Ballad

For days wind rolls in like waves
set to desiccate switch grass and thistle,
set to spread dandelion and sycamore seed heads
into garden pots and vacant lots.
Summer wind's inevitableness stirs permeance,
fondles a sure sense of what we might
become through repetition and ignition.
Let our habits make us a we
that sustains itself through searing light and birdcall
filled mornings, hang into our minds and hook
the part of us meant to escape any hold.

What We Are Never

We have never been alone in this world,
       though we sometimes think we're consecrating our solitary
              self with each day as a move into our individuality.
We are not isolate particles waiting to find
       a right rhythm nor trying to find
              a voice to speak precious thoughts.
Once we get being's hang, press those selves
       from our skins into the ensemble dancing and singing around us,
           lift voices into noise, let them rain down
                 not clean and sharp, but muddled, muted,
                        wet with other voices.

Not Felt as One But Two

Where once we bent down, listened to what beckoned us
        as more than one, now fracture
                seals in surges.

Come with us into a secure place, our voices joined;
        rivers flow from our fingers, rivers
                join with deltas, oceans—no need to distill.

Light shafts rain down on our heads with a radiance
        not felt as one but two. Kick dirt to reveal
                worms and crawling bugs that will satiate.
Fondle a leaf's ridges to get back to our knowing.
        Snap hard into a twig—peel back our new selves.

East 19th Street Elegy

Nasturtium climbed over rock and compacted soil,
   rose with clinging tendrils to our worn fence.
Up in the bottlebrush tree, thick red pipe cleaners pricked
    Bay-clean air; hummingbirds made it their mission to
      rise, fall, tunnel straight into red flowers.
At dusk a raccoon family would fix themselves in row
   on a pine's long limb before the moon stretched
     full into Oakland sky. Across the street,
        near the apartment building's entrance, veladoras religiosas
         glowed, a memorial to Hector,
            a fourteen-year-old shot on his way home one night.
The memorial flowers blown by wind would cast off petals
  —sweet drops of red, yellow, fuchsia,
     left free to purifying air, pushed away from their hold,
       set to find rest on wind's forever release.

Awakening

The window behind our bed, broken
   by a strong wind that slammed it against the house,
     swung unrepaired for a year; Bay winds
       blew it open and closed, like a lung
         flapping forward and collapsing inward.

At midnight we'd return from our kitchen shift,
   air thick with orange glow, a quietness pushed
     upon small houses, old stucco apartment buildings, car lined streets
       empty of all human traffic. We'd climb three flights
         to our attic nest, wrap ourselves in beer and weed,
           curl into our mind like an embryo
             circling in on itself, wrapping itself
               in its cord.

That window's creak lulled us to sleep;
   morning bird chants and cars whining to halt at the stop sign
       made us turn, open our eyes
         to Lake Merritt's light glare.

Until, through that open window at 3:48 am
   we heard a woman scream, run for her life
     down the hill to our right, her broken heels slapped
       sidewalk, turned onto asphalt; the pursuer's
         deep throated shout, intent on catching her,
           on stopping her flight.

Call the police. Yell at the pursuer to stop, now.
   Stop hampering our own flight.
     Get off the mind-thread's spin.
       Weave a life. Fix the window.

Live as the Tomatillo Reaches for Life on a Hot July Day

A three-month-old tomatillo, branches thickening,
bursting forth like firm poles filled
with fruit and flower—
how it rises underneath the lemon tree,
set on pulling itself toward the canopy straight
to sun—it sends fragrance
meant to fill its flowers with bees and butterflies,
bends itself until it is squat
set to take all summer can give, pull heat, light
into its body—an electric stirring towards life.

Words are No Use

Now summer's heat throbs in our hearts;
our pulse quickens until we feel a beat in each finger.
Aloe stands straight towards porch ceilings;
oleander flares near roadsides.
Each day lengthens into more of itself,
repeats itself in sureness. Warm winds
push across the valley, days and days
pollen, twig, leaf dried too early fly
into our hands, our hair, catch on roofs,
make nests in alleyways.

This is insubstantiality—this not being able to clutch
ground when everything around us repeats.
While heat ticks up, we sit on porches with gaping mouths,
unable to form words to take us to the next level,
while we pound our passion against unformed
words, get it out through our bodies after the sun
has set, one to one, words having merged,
no use to us.

Aperture

In an accelerating summer day's heat stillness,
      air breathes through sycamore leaves—
           watch its slow turn, swirl, an aroma cast back
                to our noses; roll sweetness in our mouths.
Desiccated pine needles exhale fresh oxygen
      spun from lack of car exhaust. Trucks that once
           moved steady like rail cars up and down our street
              have slowed and climb the hill
like Salmon lost in a thin mountain stream
      troubled with rocks. Silence lets
           thrush, blackbird, and warbler pitches
                penetrate our city's morning wake—each note
corresponds to the next, rises louder than human traffic,
      fills embryonic air with a wish and promise.

The Hive in Us Strives

We take our fears into our hearts, wrestle
   still with any give into the other.
What loss will it take for us to move
   full flush into erasing borders,
      our sentences merging,
         our clauses' fusion uninterrupted by punctuation?
Mycelia lengthens by inches each day,
   its subterranean tendrils curl, cling
      to become miles of network,
         join oak, tomatillo, fig root,
            create digestion and nutrient absorption,
               leap over obstacles to grow, amass over distance,
                  create bridges and bridges between.

Destiny's Garment

Find evidence for our devotion
as it rings from a grape leaf's veins,
shouts from cardinal flowers' red tips,
tunnels through cracked earth to vibrate
with red worms and nematodes.
Spores flush on a plum's surface
        could fill us with awe; a clover's sudden sprouting in a field
              could make us shake with the will to dance.
Creative tension pulls us into pressure;
    let growth curl into our palms
        as they grip promise's ballot, its sign, our stem.

Shrouded Silence's Heat

What if we're lovers, turned so far
into loving the other that we turn
away towards anything but the familiar,
leave a love's known safety,
push it away from ourselves
into desiccating post-solstice air,
only for longing to embolden, slip
like mud through our fingers to arc around
our hearts and grow and grow and overtake
all ending thoughts, to mold new ways
of resurrecting in the heat as it fills
every empty place with seeds
that emerge and emerge, unstoppable
in shrouded silence's heat?

The Joining

Enclosed by houses, bars, warehouses,
in our small city garden greens grow
to untold heights. Trombetta squash
sounds itself on our gutter,
corn reaches towards sycamore with yellow flower tassels.
With thumb and index finger, I pluck, pluck,
harvest, harvest until my hands stain green,
fragrant with life's pulse, until emerald veins
dig into mine and begin to move through my blood,
throb with a wish to grow, inch their way
into my heart, my brain, convert me to another form
meant to extend and lengthen, overtake
human objects like our house, our fence, our roof.
When my belly rumbles with the need for breakfast
I return to my human form,
my thoughts filled with eggs, sausage,
greens covered in olive oil.
At night, restless with duties, obligations,
I escape into the radicchio's, lettuce's, arugula's
water pull, feel a pressure pulse
draw life from beyond my ankles, my toes,
reach into bed sheets for dirt, loam, humus,
to make me more than a jumble of human thoughts,
make words form between stretching synapses,
make syllables drop from my open lips,
make meaning become firm,
transmittable, capable of being emitted.

Put summer into these lines

in hope that it will be tracked
        into our heads, unable to split off into autumn's
                sink into winter, unable to be threshed,
                        dissected, cleaned for the table's harvest.
Let the zenith be still within us;
        let noon's no shadow
                contain any thoughts of dissipation.
Let energy light veins in a wish
        to cover, grow in full fecundity,
                in forgetfulness of seasonal slips.
Put summer into these synapses,
        set to snap and spark ideas, ideas,
                set to propel us long into life's steady hum.

Each Tremble Becomes an Earthquake

The highway's noise, inaudible most nights,
in July's breeze mixes in a syncopation,
joins with the light-rail.
What will we turn ourselves towards,
with suggestions and predictable directions urging this and that;
what will make us maintain ourselves,
sure on what is right and how to do it—
how not to turn into comfort or agreement's shallow root,
not consent to be dulled to a cactus needle's prick.
The needle calls us to join in dissent, rage, fierce opposition
to any tearing or rupture from our purpose.
Rise, disparate but whole, announce
our division and make it drive us
round as one of many faces
transmuted; speak the message that we
will not stand apart while others suffer.
        The network splits off,
                but each tremble becomes an earthquake
                      shattering, shaking, pulling,
                            erecting an us.

Autumn and Embracing a Never Wane

Driving into the Sierra,
        we lean toward autumn with its long shadows,
                thin, transparent light that shines through fire smoke.
Aspens and sycamores have a yellow tinge,
        blackberries turn sticky with seeds,
                cool morning pushes towards afternoon.
Sleepiness etches itself from protests
        that jumped with change-fueled energy.
Under shaded trees, crickets raise their healing voices in dissipating light.
        Never given to embracing negative narratives,
                we shake ourselves to wholeness.

Time Reverses While We Sleep

Every night full flush with summer's cricket and traffic ticks,
our minds run and leap over obstacles of money, work, to do lists
heaped on our laps. Our minds' edges push
until we can't see ourselves as distinct anymore,
until we don't know what happened then
or what we felt like once when we knew something.
Now we know nothing more and more;
what we don't know sits with us through sleeplessness.
We're adventurers discovering places
we've been to—maybe we didn't look close enough
before, taste enough, listen enough
while we met this or that person,
moved through this scene to that.
What we don't know
increases with each decade, hurls itself
toward our closed eyes, flings that part of us
with knowledge from bed, and we are transfixed
with ignorance, thankful that we can begin
to know the world again, start from nothing
again, remake
everything from nothing.

Ash Flakes Linger like Substantial Fragments

Ash flakes fall like snow, litter our garden pots,
        catch in fine spider webs spread over soil
                surface, linger like substantial fragments,
                        like ghosts of our forests, our hillsides, like pieces
of world now gone, still there to remind us,
        to tell us to change, transform
                into that next version of ourselves,
                      become ones who stop
                              causing and causing ignition.

Smoked Summer

Smoke thick like fog blankets our valley,
    Creates a quiet cover that muffles cars and conversations.
Ash falls, our snow in August, our new particle
    To filter, wear masks against.
Stay inside, stay in safe air,
    Turn from window panes towards computers, TVs, dogs.
No more single-track trails snaking along the river's path;
    No more wading in cool reservoir released water.
Someday soon we'll have naturally smoked olives, plums,
    Turn ash into our soil so plants have carbon to grow,
        Croon towards a clear sky, bring forth
            Fruit from once stunted blossoms.

Queens of La Luna Bella

On Baker Beach we, queens for the year,
wrote letters of love to our young selves
that bloomed from our breasts and thighs.
We made our minds open sourced to the microscopic lives
that swam around our naked bodies, ran full thrust
into the Pacific to let its salty rush crush us with its cleansing
love savor. At night, while crickets sang
in Golden Gate Park's branches curled by wind and fog,
we drummed and based nights, danced high
towards an unseen light in clubs,
etched a new narrative from our almost full
female selves' crumble. Years would take us up,
up to where we could name our wholeness, grip it with our
teeth, howl to La Luna Bella with an earthquake force.

Conflagration

Conflagration in our roots
        spurs ignition after ignition
destroys and concocts
        so many manifestations of us
that each one as it forms
        jumps back into the blaze,
remade, reformed as if wood
        we come from, as if fuel for fire
churns in our bones—
        our bones sticks
meant to be turned over, transferred,
        our formations torn down, rebuilt, melted away,
only to emerge rich charcoal,
        ready to give the land what it needs to grow.

In our roots, conflagration
        sends us out of ourselves,
leaves worms writhing deep
        close to our bulk, burrowing through
our substance. What sparks
        we have; watch us flare and set all obstacles
in motion. We mustn't
        let break ways stop us,
we must not let our flames
        fizz out, must not let
our substance wither away,
        must fill ourselves again and again,
must find a way to flare,
        grow larger and collect
more and more, not let
        a pulling in
be a pushing away.

Love's Perpetual Birth

Breathe in air wet with grass's growth, frog proliferation,
    red mud offering itself after a summer's thunder rain.
In the fields, mice scurry to harvest bugs
    lifted down from rain drops that pelted their scales.
A cleanness moves from the Blue Ridge over Mom and Dad's house,
    an airing of that which used to make us sad,
        a leaving of old grudges now frees us to love and love,
           to not get hung up on words, to not care
               about precision in caring.
The pond reflects Southern Magnolia and maple,
    rosemary grows year-round on the stone wall's south side,
        and the compost pile, rich from years of chicken poo,
           steams and steams through each season,
               fills our noses with decomposition, regrowth,
                  perpetual birth, sweetness.

Filter, Dissolve, Cut, Cycle

Fog's tiny particles filter what sunlight gives:
diffuse into switch grass blades,
cut into pasture's rise,
enclose us from sun sear,
cycle us back
to push through caked soil,
set to emerge.

Concoct

Let the history of you go, let yourself
        create new vocabulary, name your self
                as one of the many ways one can be.
Winds that push marsh spears
        mold you. Rains that become fine points
                dissolve you. Snows melt, freeze, and crack you
                        new forms. Every hand that plugs into you,
                      every eye that meets yours,
                                  every prick of loss that pains,
                                      every finger that presses
                                  into your mind,
turns you over, makes you lose yourself enough
        to narrate, rewrite, spring and spin
                new letters toward the edges
                        of what sizzles, snaps, concocts a human.

No Stop-Time

Everything always grows,
   always moves forward.
      In winter, grasses root, build their extensions
         to ready for spring sun's stun.
On cold days, with light so low we can hardly perceive it,
   mycelia push their networks below our feet,
      travel miles towards moisture,
         make their presence known through soil layers.
The myth of stopping, rest's false
   understanding, pulls us forward
      to put one finger in front of another,
         create from the invisible
            a castle to hang our minds on,
               etch rivers we can travel to reinvent, weave
               a new scene, grow new roots
                  that pull us down in regeneration.

Bildungsroman

I left the DC suburbs in an old Toyota, cigarette butts
in the ashtray, fingers stained with tar, my long hair
twisting in the Appalachian wind. Terrified inside,
but I had to begin my journey,
move forward into an unknown that screamed to me from pages.
End of land sadness, Kerouac wrote in a book I underlined
every other word in. To be alone on an adventure, to leave and leave until
you find yourself, the "you" apart from family, comfort, conditions;
the eye of the writing self that screams at you in the night to speak
to move forward, to not be afraid
of experience, to not be afraid of being alone.

The red stone dust and spires of southern Utah spun
in dry air, little insects snapped at my knees,
dragonflies buzzed about my eyes, unsteadying them.
From the base of Navajo Mountain, I pulled myself
from a cocoon and began to walk, kicked up dust,
ate fried bread and canned green beans re-purposed
from the Gulf War to the Indian Boarding School's cafeteria.

A hunger grew, wrapped itself around my ankles,
moved them forward step-by-step into the desert canyon.
Sagebrush waved; rattlesnakes swam in red dust.
Walk into the next version, sweat into the new, almost adult you.
Soft skin melted down into a dry earth;
my brain cracked open to think what I might be like unhinged.
I inhabited crevices and pockets where rain
once pounded depressions into sandstone.
A woodpecker with its hook
hammered our remix on a mesquite's thick bark–
grasshopper ticks became our drum.
Tracks from the last truck that passed on this road hours ago
became my route home to another me.

Mural, Balmy Alley, San Francisco

Turn from cactus flowers to needle pricks to streams
rushing forward, our feet set firm in death.
We fight and lash; machines
that we have been trained to love
turn us into the ground.
Everything once unownable, owned.
Everything that once set us free we're chained to:
water damned and controlled in irrigation canals;
a price for water, gas, wind, sun's energy.
Our minerals mined and exported to serve human progress machines—
our eyes bleed at what has been stolen
to be sold back.

Rise to Elevation

      Walking up the hill, elevation 2,543 feet, my lungs fill and fill with only minor creaks and cramps. Snow the night before left white shock and ice crystals on oaks and switchgrass, freezing tree bones, pine fingers in snow.

      Four days ago, the ultrasound set on a thyroid nodule showed light beams that bounced and bounced as the sonographer rolled the machine's sensor over my throat again and again.

      What light can do; what light waves can reveal.

      What we hide from is growth here.

      No growth prayers.

      Counter to my always urge, my always wish: grow, grow, grow—never stop.

      What prayers I have started since aging.

      Two years ago, a benign nodule in the apex of my left lung jolted into a CT scan, momentarily shattering the images I had of mountain climbing, of clear runner's lungs.

      Every year, turn away from California's forest fires and into the house with five air filters.

      Every year, I pray for walking up hill after hill, to never have to stop climbing hills, to always be able to feel tension build in my ribs, always be able to hold air in.

      Pine needles pull snow crystals

      Puncture our air cages

      Spin us into elevation rise

      Don't live in fear; don't retreat to the potential loss of self. Make up belief that everything will be fine. Take sea salt with iodine on sweet potatoes, eat oysters and cod, run or walk every day, no more than one glass of red wine, no more than one cup of coffee, no more than one life to live.

Water's Benediction

Watch each raindrop fall,
        spin left, hurl forward
                toward parked cars, lavender spires, plucked olive trees.

Count each drop, pull its concentration in,
        imagine what it can do as life force's one token,
                a life's weight.

Let drops build, build, gather, gather
        onto sidewalk asphalt, dirt patches, greenspaces;
                let water's benediction bathe everything
                        in potential to move, accumulate, raise.

Swallows' Calls Rising

In summer's heat, swallows' calls rising
from sycamore and ash's tented leaves
make me want to grip him close,
get rid of clothes' traffic,
word and shoe congestion,
feel his heartbeat throughout his body,
how when it thumps his chest hairs
tremble, how when the air conditioner
rides after its recent gust of coolness,
the skin above his eyebrows releases sweat beads,
how skin to skin wetness marks our contact spots,
while the cars slow at stop signs and speed up,
gain momentum as they leave our neighborhood.
Crickets start toward one another
in dryness as sun pitches low;
heat to heat, we flare,
burn any impediment to fusion.

Ripe in Our Apex

Rain drop sputter
Assemble our fragments
Pull ourselves in
Rake it baby
Cull each part
Whole. Any hiding part,
Any loss of self
Will be gained back, revealed.
What parts of ourselves
Have we hidden, turned over
In our toes and minds?
Grip each fragment
To ring in a wholeness,
Set forth fruit that we'll bear home,
Fork into, taste explode in our mouths
Like a fig ripe in summer's apex.

Diverge from Difference's Narrative

Whatever shelter setting yourself apart served,
                              made skin soft, pliable, punctured
                              with any turn of words. Little girls
made fun of by other little girls and boys turn into themselves,
                              curl so tight that nothing penetrates,
not even what they want to get in can:
                              hands' warm pressure, syllables driven
                              from union
spin off a hardened body, wipe themselves
                              off the mind's aperture, shut.
What can carry us through doesn't take sides,
                              doesn't think of his or hers, theirs or ours,
                              this or that;
to only connect, to join,
                              that's our ignition into the world.

Rust New Forms

Let's ride the wind's deep current, let air's rift pull us
From congestion and division's build.
In the space inside us, between us,
Let's ride boundaries, crest edges that puncture, cleave,
Let the cages we've erected around ourselves
Get blown apart, lifted, ridden until they're just broken pieces
Left to rust us new forms.

Image Focus

    The thin biopsy needle slides in and out of my thyroid, an organ I learned about in 4th grade anatomy but forgot about. Last week I didn't even know it was in my neck. In the fluorescent-lighted room, coldness that is every hospital room and doctor's office, air's staleness, I prayed and imagined a hillside that I looked at every afternoon when I was 19 at an internship at Thomas Jefferson's Center for Historic Plants.

    With a Camel Wide Mouth in my soil smudged fingers and between my lips, I watched the summer afternoon's thunderstorms move east. The air's sudden stillness, hay and cedar's fresh scent made its way into me. I imagined large rats climbing from their holes and through hillside's rolling grasses.

    Whatever was before me at that time, whatever future I would move towards, whatever would happen in my life, I told myself I could always come back to this place, a stillness, a pause, smells of life coming forward into themselves, into possibility.

    The needle goes in and out, sharp rings of pain move from my neck and then dissipate. What force a little needle can bring.

    A hillside, hay tips browning in August, wet with rain's pounding, tiny plants underneath weeds birthing forward into lightning's danger, a honeysuckle vine's fragrant spill.

    Room lights, blanched tile, doctor's gloved hand, hill, thunderclouds, hay tips waving, thrown back against themselves, still growing, still forming seeds, inching forward toward an after-storm sun's cloudy brightness.

Channel the Void's Roar
After Michelle, After Baldwin's "Sonny's Blues"

There's something one can do with suffering,
   a way to fill the void that keeps sweeping,
      sweeping you forward in its spinning
      chasm. Feel the pull to pick up the glass,
      turn away from steadying yourself,
         wrap yourself away from anyone
            who would try to steal that false salve
               that ends up sealing you into the void's constant suck.
Pull yourself away, make it from your mind's tunnel,
   a constant falling, to a new way of being in this world,
   make it to imagine what life is like without the ever-dissolving bandage.
Make it farther and further,
   ignore gravity's build and rumble below the void's aperture.
      Don't let the void's vacuum take your toes,
         tug at your hips, draw in your fingernails
            —your hands will not stop
               clenching at walls and flesh for buoyancy.
Don't be taken.
   Tune in with a shaking draw, let it rumble from its depths.
Listen to notes of dissonance, pay attention
   to how they roar in certain spaces, echo emotions;
      send them for others to hear—ping notes with words,
         hang thinning minds on meaning in syllables,
         walk with the void's lessons for living.

Pitch Words, Pitch Our Minds

Interstate hum roars in wind.
We stay near the house, to leave is bad luck,
wandering in light, we might wither,
dry like thinning grasses left to grow long in vacant lots.
Wandering in darkness, we might grow fat
on moon curvature, make ourselves full
on its pull's romance promise.

We can never think of what to say,
nothing ever says, we pitch words
under soil clods, pitchfork
our minds towards what we hope
can slide inside of another.

Don't Stop

Whatever reason we have to check
                into oblivion, whatever hurt we try
to kick from our minds,
                let it not destroy us, let us not kill ourselves
quickly with a bullet or pill or slowly,
                liquor and smoke clogged. Tunnel into soil,
let our fingers rub tiny pebbles' coolness,
                sift through fine sand, heavy clay clumps, worms wet
with last night's rain. Pull weeds
                that sicken the plants we eat, let wind roll over
what we grow. The struggle with force
                makes leaf flesh firmer, tastier. Don't stop
                planting, don't stop germinating seeds,
                let our fruits fill us, fat with life, bloated
                with what can make us whole.

Elegy for Her Promise

What starkness rests in a childhood friend's death.
How innocent we were, we'll always be.
No sad end, no breaking your brain
with vodka and stairs takes away from your promise:

                    You, pigtailed girl in roller skates,
                          coasted around our cul-de-sac.
Towering tulip poplars behind our houses rose tall;
    we'd gather their fallen flowers in our mothers' coffee mugs.
We used to wade barefoot in puddles,
          search for tadpoles to cup in our small hands.
                  One thousand fifty-two frogs pumped
                          their throats in Rock Creek Park's wet cover.

How perfect the brownie cake
from your Barbie Easy Bake Oven tasted in our mouths.
We ate cake after cake on your driveway's downslope
—our lip sides chocolate covered.
Satiation made us happy kids.

To the Homeless Man Asleep Across the Street

What tenderness each curl brings,
                      what thoughts of a baby's head
                                    slick with afterbirth, just formed.
His bare arm around his head,   hands withered by sun, street smudge,
                              days on the sidewalk and grass strip.
              Dirt digs into his nails.
His jeans gather to commas,
              his eyelids, soft wrinkles thinning
                      to slits—pure lenses.
His ears, burned with sun,   sunken by hate slurs, spin
                            transformation, foot fall's
                            promise, sun's red rise.

Walk Ourselves Free

Awaken to sudden sadness and impatience.
Walk the dog, walk ourselves free from our mind's
trap. Small finch, feathers still birth soft, fuzzy,
fly, barely land on a myrtle limb near our ears.
Energy snap of wings, impatient to beak-grip
leaf, flower, ant, small moth
—spring to pine, out of vision.

Second Berry Harvest

Watch the strawberry's redness turn;
just plucked from a thread held to leaf crown,
watch it draw in edges
flush until crimson shines.

Accumulate hours underneath building light,
day's crest giving into night, amassing heat
that slowly gathers, pulls toward fruiting.

Sweetness and acidity dance on our tongue,
bring a new meaning of awakening
—how dew drop and rain cascade
drawn through to center crown
express clarity, emergence
of water, sun, night rest, soil essence,
a mouth's gift.

From the Powered Center

What does the hummingbird
Say as it accelerates through smoke-scented air?
What mission does the mantis move toward
As it crawls over pine bark to treetop?
Losses never stack up if we reinvent them into gains;
Our new versions spin us into us.

Like bees moving into a sunflower,
Like worms diving through leaf litter,
Like aphids convening in their pepper leaf feeding,
We devour our sustaining parts,
Turn away from what could dissolve
An us, what could interrupt the bond.
Our bodies like battery inverters,
Not charged on the other, but on ourselves,
We each fuel our propulsion toward the other,
Set on gain, accumulation, movement
From the powered center.

Stretch In Ascension

Autumn's wind moves smoke away,
Clears soot on a lilac's broad leaf,
Blows in breaths we take
As if we'd been held under water for too long
Only for our buoyancy to propel us forward
Into air's healing capacity.

Woodpeckers coast from pine to pine,
Make quick work of acorns,
Their wings small machines pumping into winter's dance,
Their beaks hammers set to make sustenance
Carry them forward for spring's food promise.

We make plans again, firm in our insistence
That what we sowed will nourish us,
Will bring us more into each other
Without losing our center.

Each acorn, its hull and husk edge burned,
Sets to tunnel into our field, root down
With microbes, take all nutrients
Through its incipient body to rain
Tall over grasses, stretch us and itself
In ascension, catch potential.

Beach Day

Waves circle themselves, fold
before sandy arcs jut into ocean. A crab's claw,
a mussel's backside, a sand dollar's round edge
—all pieces meant to pull us into day's embrace.
        What losses we've nursed on our way to a firm holding?
            What edges of ourselves did we turn away from?
Each leap into sand sends us to new heights,
our feet sink in sand only to lift higher,
breathe in more of gestating ocean's
life kiss and shadow kill.
        How much does happiness
                rely on our feet shift, our mind's turn, our lungs
                      capacity to open into possibility's vastness?
Ocean claws cliff, begs steep slope to return,
        fold back in massive wave movement,
            knocks us into a new bliss
                    formerly unseen by our myopic visions.

Summon Sheets That Will Swallow Dryness

A calmness, a settling nudges each leaf to sidewalk.
        Summer's heat and smoke blows past pine-studded mountains.
What can we do when silence gets thrown at us, when the summer's
        Harvest promise runs us bare in October,
When what we've tried to love and sow has us digging in dirt,
        Fingernails to dry dust, palms to warm rocks?
Our city's sidewalk tells us one foot equals two, that on our corners,
        Nourishment waits in duck-fat fries,
Organic strawberry smoothies, grass-fed burgers.

If we stare straight down the street from its center,
        Palm and sycamore, curb and cars, yellow lines all align,
        Leap over the hill towards downtown.
Ride alignment until the pattern becomes a habit in our heads.
Follow symmetry to reap our seeds' growth.
Forget smoke and desiccation, think rain drops.
Summon sheets that will cascade on our heads,
            Tangle in our hair, swallow dryness in their wake.

No Escape Needed

Sycamore leaves curl like injured palms.
        Broken Crown Royal bottles smashed against dusty fences
                Edge front lawns. Yet the doves still crowd on myrtle,
      Still dive into our pepper plants to peck
              Unripe fruits, forage for seed from the neighbor's feeder.

Our backyards, once spaces forgotten by commutes, extended work hours,
                      Now flourish in their flowering, leap
Tall into our smoked air, collect each drop
                We sparingly set on soil, become freedom
Gateways in our minds, making us limitless in how we approach
                Each leaf that unfolds longer and longer.
Raised beds map trails and roads   We could take away
                            From our computer cloud meetings,
                            Away from ties that bind and free.
Look into the leaf's underbelly,
        Trace protruding veins to fine fissures,
                Find imagination that allows us to be anywhere.

End of the Fire Season, End of the Dry Season Ode

Drainage ponds drying grip
      last season's last drops against their edges,
            let mallow grow tall in smoked air.
Blackberries crowd seasonal creeks, sip enough
      liquid energy to drop berries no one harvests;
            drupelets hang, lean towards dry soil, quartz, burned branches.
On mountain fire roads, tall pines that have stood five years
         after bases and bark charred
         fall, break in pieces; their center wood soft,
            bug and fungus food set to nourish until November's rain.
We preserved ourselves through barrenness,
      sustained pepper, tomato, squash harvests,
         waited through 106-degree days
            with smoke sitting on our hills, shifting into our valleys.
What dryness we have now.
      What measures we've taken to keep
         our internal pilot lights lit through our barrenness.
Not lost in what we look for,
      like little worms trying this and that soft patch of soil,
         searching for the sink and pull
         full into water-willed microbes, decaying oak leaves.
What will we do with water when it comes?
      What canals, what reservoirs will we build
         to hold so much liquid fuel
         that we never forget saturation, penetration, proliferation,
         that we get so wet that all our dirtiness, dust, debris
      empty into our streams and bays, purify us
         with knowledge of how
            we have yet to be.

Suddenness

We churn ourselves through oak trees
      leaf-stripped in mid-winter,
           through burned tree stumps.
Hills roll towards us, cast
      leafless pine tree tips through our legs' veins.
Our feet once grounded by rainless soil
      now sink in red mud to white roots,
           to grasses untouched by light.
Young star thistle push from clay soil;
      birth points open and open,
           spread thin, yield wide
                in blue mountain sky suddenness.

Gabrielle is a writer, professor, and former chef. Her memoir, *Hive-Mind*, details her time of love, awakening, and tragic loss on an organic farm. Her first and second poetry books, *Too Many Seeds* (2021) and *Break Self: Feed* (2024), are published by Finishing Line Press. Her poetry has been published in the *Atlanta Review, Evergreen Review, Adirondack Review, San Francisco Public Press, Fourteen Hills, pacificREVIEW, Connecticut River Review, Catamaran, Borderlands: Texas Poetry Review, Sand Hills, University of Alabama's Al Dente, Cathexis Northwest Press, Folio,* and *American Poetry Review*. Gabrielle is the Farm-to-Fork columnist for Inside Sacramento magazine: https://insidesacramento.com/sacramento-dining/farm-to-fork/ Access links to her memoir, poetry books, farm-to-fork articles, published works, and interviews through her website: www.gabriellemyers.com

www.ingramcontent.com/pod-product-compliance
Lightning Source LLC
Chambersburg PA
CBHW030056170426
43197CB00010B/1552